All About FLAMINGOS

Krista Conway
Copyright 2022

All rights reserved.

Two flamingos met
on the beach.

They smiled when
they saw each other.

"Hello! I'm
Pinky. It's so nice to meet you! I'm here
looking for something to eat. Have you
seen any shrimp today?"

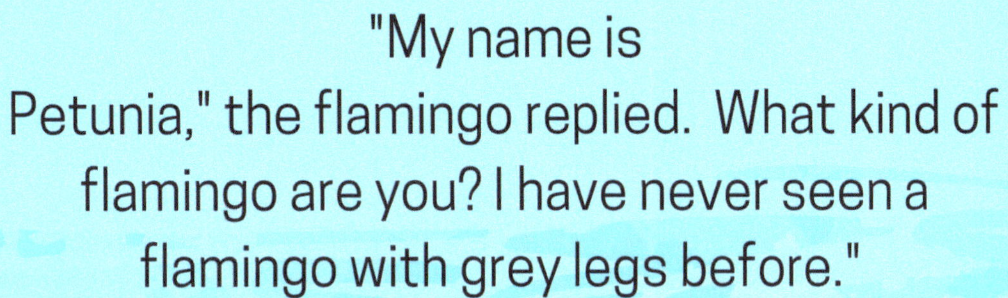

"My name is
Petunia," the flamingo replied. What kind of
flamingo are you? I have never seen a
flamingo with grey legs before."

With a smile he said, "I am a Chilean flamingo. I'm here to find something to eat as well. I'm hungry for a some algae and fish."

The two flamingos looked for their favorite foods together. They used the lamellae in their special bill to filter-feed their favorite algae, small fish, shrimp, and insects. They were both happy and full when they returned to the beach.

"Did you know you'll be taller than me one day Petunia?" Petunia looked shocked to hear the news.

Pinky, the Chilean flamingo understood. It wasn't that long ago that he was just a chick himself. "I was grey when I was a chick."

As he thought about his color as a chick, he remembered that he was very small compared to his parents.

"It took almost three years to get my pink feathers, but I was okay with that. I enjoyed swimming around and watching the other flamingos fly."

Just then a lesser flamingo flew over. "That's a lesser flamingo," Pinky exclaimed. "They have black flight feathers."

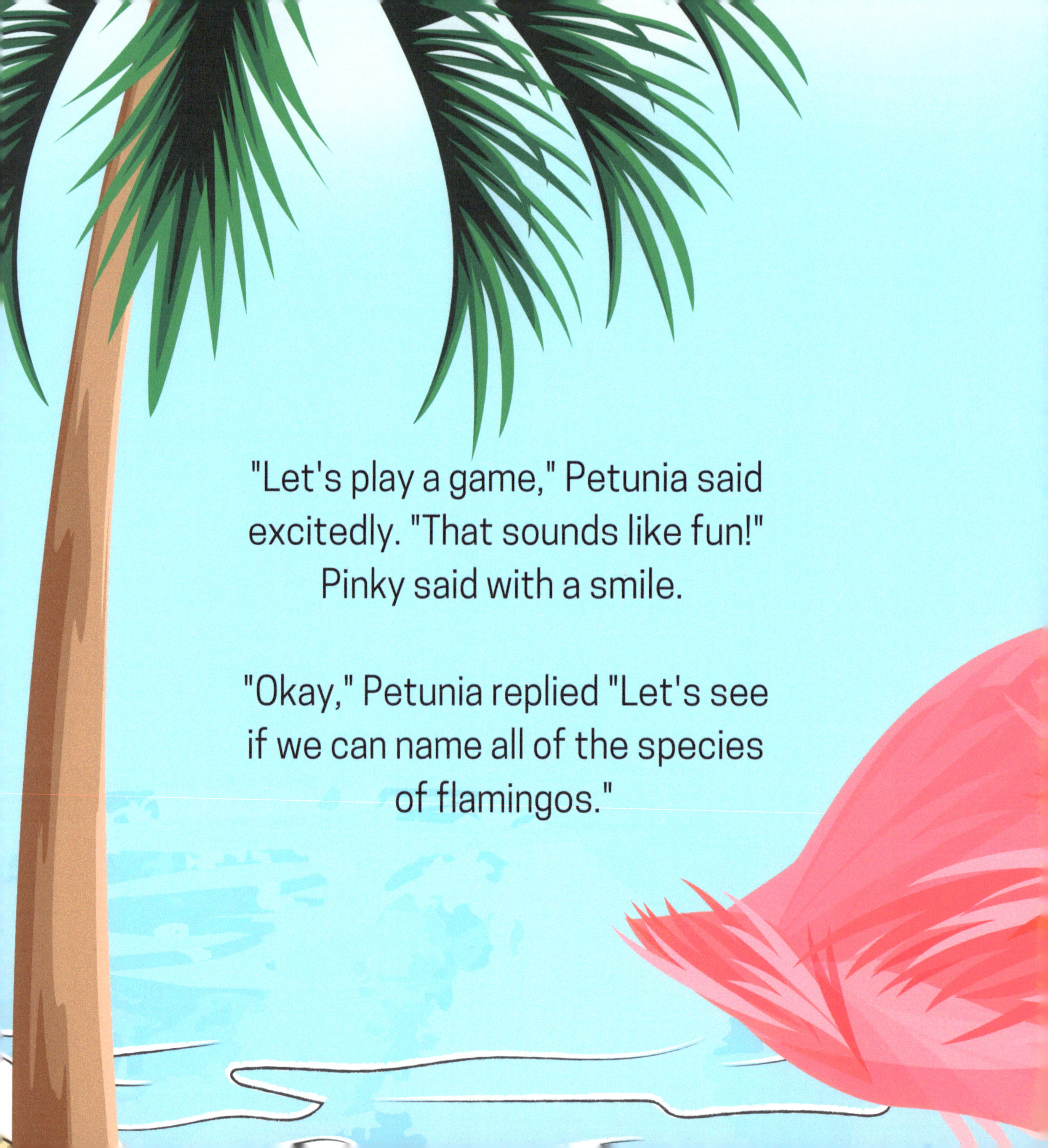
"Let's play a game," Petunia said excitedly. "That sounds like fun!" Pinky said with a smile.

"Okay," Petunia replied "Let's see if we can name all of the species of flamingos."

Pinky looked up at the sky and said "I am a greater flamingo, you're a Chilean flamingo and we just watched a lesser flamingo fly over. There are three other species we're missing."

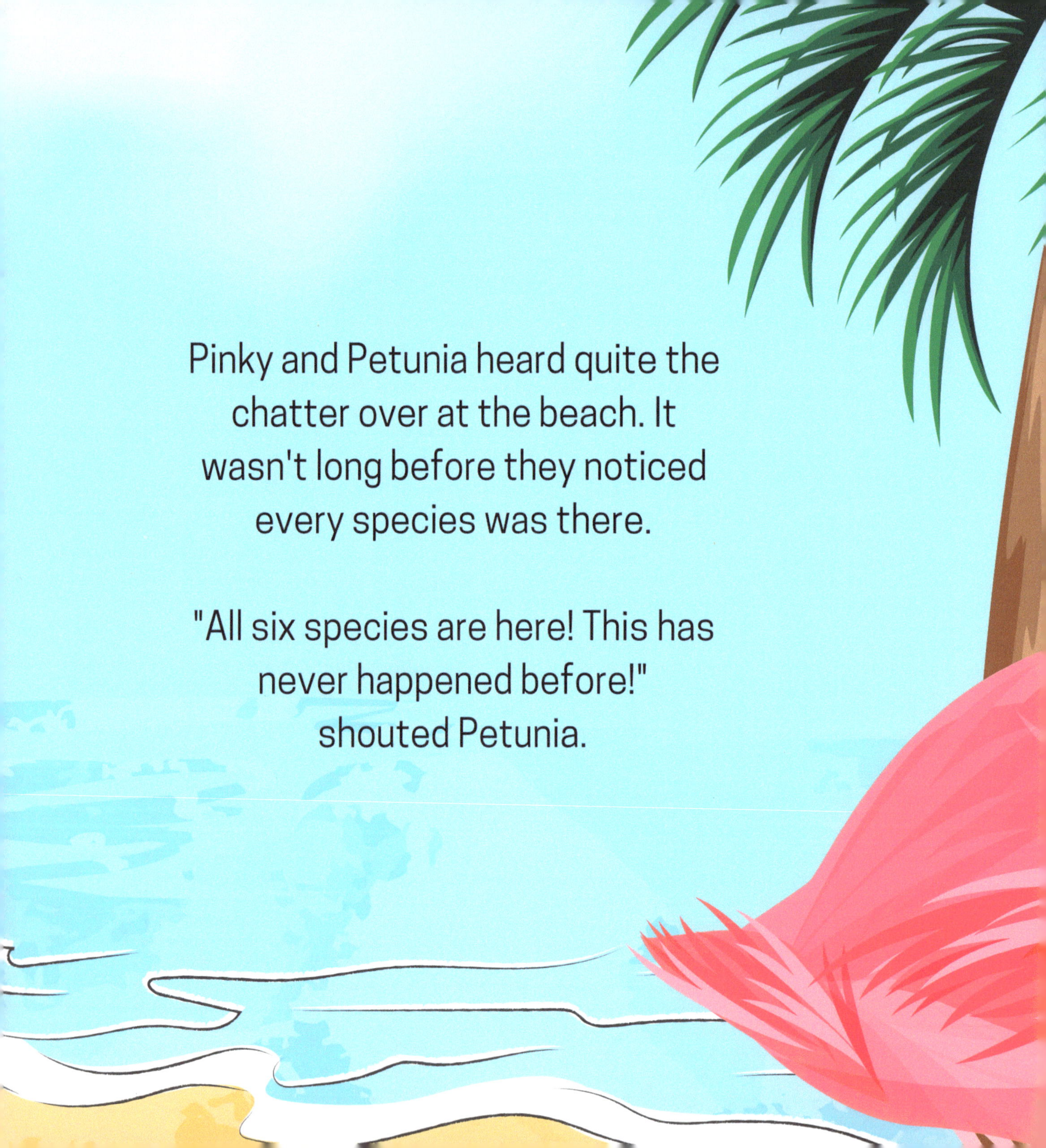

Pinky and Petunia heard quite the chatter over at the beach. It wasn't long before they noticed every species was there.

"All six species are here! This has never happened before!" shouted Petunia.

"And will most likely never happen again," said Pinky.

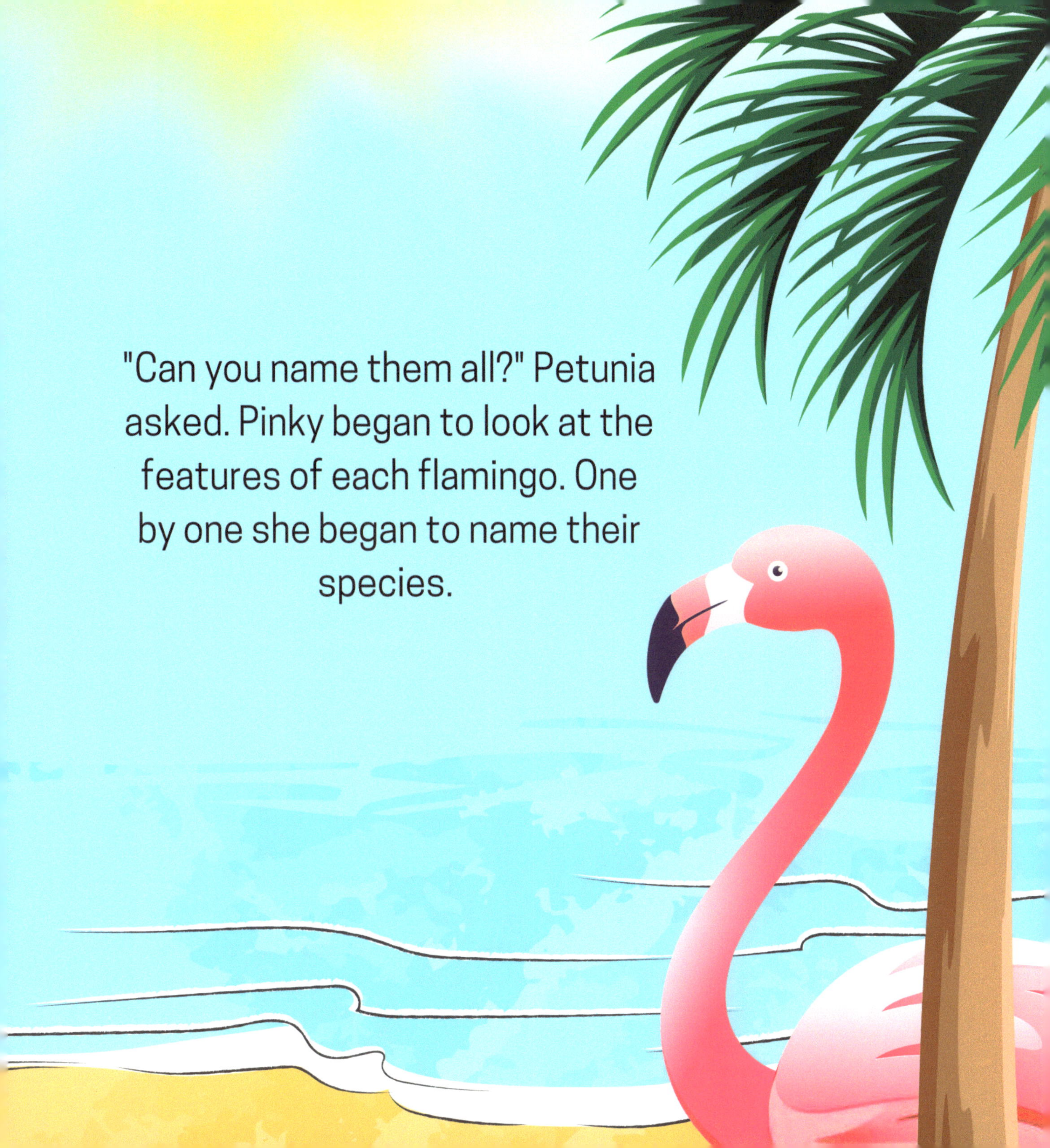

"Can you name them all?" Petunia asked. Pinky began to look at the features of each flamingo. One by one she began to name their species.

Greater
Flamingo
Chilean
Flamingo
Lesser Flamingo

James' Flamingo
Caribbean Flamingo
Andean Flamingo

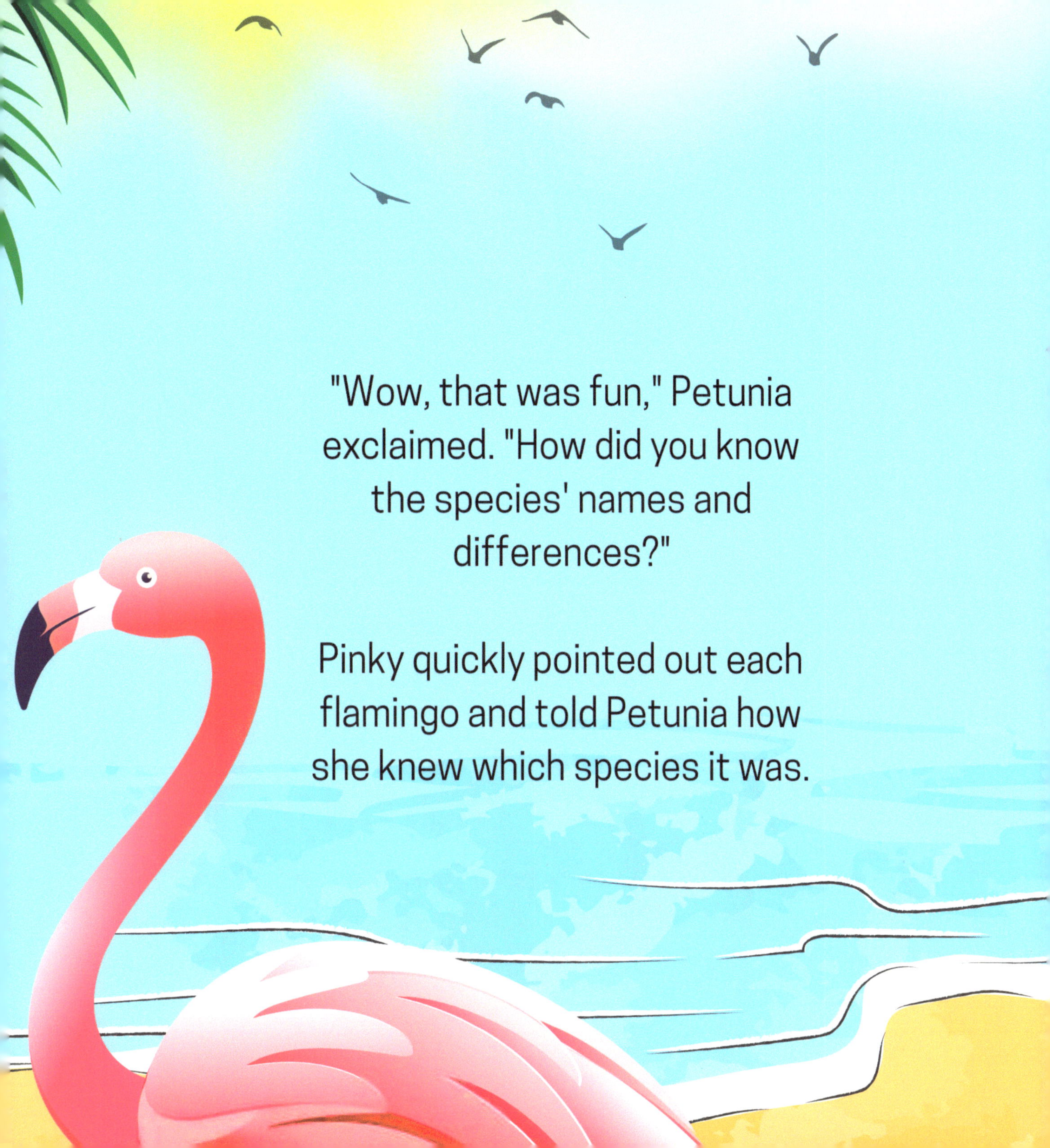

"Wow, that was fun," Petunia exclaimed. "How did you know the species' names and differences?"

Pinky quickly pointed out each flamingo and told Petunia how she knew which species it was.

The only species with grey legs.
The tallest with the largest wing span.
Brighter than the greater flamingo.

A short, stubby bill,
red legs and eyes as adults.

The brightest
flamingo.

The only species
with yellow legs.
They also have
black flight
feathers.

As the sun began to set, Pinky and Petunia knew it was time to head home. They had both flown really far to get here and were tired from their journey.

Pinky turned one last time to Petunia and said "Want to plan to meet again next year?"

"Same time, same place," she said.